Sunshine Blooms and Haiku

www.snehasundaram.com

sunshine.haiku@gmail.com

ISBN: 978-0-578-60174-8

Illustrations and cover design by Unmesh Nayak

Sunshine Blooms and Haiku

SNEHA SUNDARAM

CONTENTS

AND SUDDENLY SPRING

waiting for you
to make the first move
cherry blossoms

spring rain
the baby finch bathes
in cherry blossoms

also stretching
in the afternoon sun
queen anne's lace

long walks
seeking in the lotus bud
Buddha

cherry blossoms
on the park bench
in memoriam

how can
you contain me
bougainvillea blooms

sotto voce*
when almond blossoms
fall

* (Italian) in a quiet voice

stretching
to make ends meet
mockingbird

ashes to ashes
a green leaf
still sprouts

piggy bank
my daughter gathers
cherry blossoms

layer
    after layer
        after layer
            spring hides in a peony

.

sunken pier
the migrating bird
wonders why

lunch rush
finding at sakura's* feet
a full moment

* (Japanese) cherry blossoms

first love
the swallow's song
calls you

baby shower
suddenly the hydrangeas bloom
blue

nesting swans
the house we built
many years ago

migrating geese
does anyone ask you
to go back

spring cleaning…
I store your memories
in Ziplock

the full moon
peaks through the clouds
a lotus blooms

in the heart
of a blooming violet
unspoken desire

so what
if you clip my wings
bonsai blooms

in cherry blossoms
the monk finds
himself

chasing shadows
the dandelion blows
away

how quickly
they grow up -
soap bubbles

first point of Aries
swans search for their reflections
in cherry blossoms

.

SUMMER'S LONGING

summer's longing
the sky and the sea
meet everyday

a big wave
chases away a little one
mating season

heatwave
following the beads of sweat
down your neck

borders
in the sand
wash them away

fishing village
the smell of the sea
on grandpa's shirt

skipping stones
three eddies away
from yesterday

red skies
the seagull tries to swallow
the sun

perigee moon
wave after wave after wave
of unsaid promises

prickly heat
even our shadows
grow apart

jugalbandi*
the sparrows
harmonize

* (Hindi) a duet in Indian classical music

long afternoon
my eyelids carry the weight
of honeysuckle

waiting
to be kissed again
sea pebbles

jetlag
the parrots win
every time

summer vacation
even the sun jumps
into the ocean

winding road
the sea sneaks up
silently

call to prayer
the myna skips

.

.

a beat

sunbathing
the baby seal
flips over

Sneha Sundaram

long summer
the dog returns
my scowl

quivering quill
the seagull splatters
my canvas

message in a bottle
the sea rejects
everything

still filling
the room you left
night blooming jasmine

urban jungle
the pigeons are also
mating

journeys
inward and out
a water lily blooms

gently swaying
to the rhythm of your breath
desert willow

the break of dawn
a butterfly flutters
into being

FIRST RAIN

carrying
the weight of raindrops
evensong

morning rush
the earthworm
just escapes

staccato
the thunder following
our silences

both a blessing
and a prayer
gulmohar blooms

finding the key
in the Myna's song
raindrops

storm clouds
the sea gathers
itself

too soon
the tide ebbs
seven-year itch

skype call
at least the raindrops
touch you

adrift
in the eye of the storm
another storm

jumping puddles
nowadays we run inside
when it rains

Rosetta stone
your fingers
find mine

Inhaling and exhaling
the monsoon winds
my accordion plays itself

distant thunder
the peacock braces
himself

let go
the wind knows the way
home

caught
in the rigmarole
a rainbow

temple bells ring
the sea still echoes
in the conch

gentle
on the leaves
a dewdrop

morning fog
the mountain goat senses
my company

instantly slipping
into old patterns
childhood home

swaying
between darkness and light
a moth

dancing in the rain
every river flows
into the sea

traffic jam
sometimes my tongue
escapes

drifting
between now and then
koel's song

remember
she spoke softly
paper boat race

still
on the mountain top
first rain

WHEN AUTUMN SINGS

harvest song
errant kites cut
the chords

wabi sabi*
the last leaf
in autumn

* (Japanese) beauty in imperfection

old diary
the pressed flower
slowly fades

full moon
I stare at my phone
it stares back

gathering mushrooms
grandmother's basket still holds
all of her secrets

back to school
my grandson explains
yolo

autumn song
on the bare hillock
fireflies dance

day light savings
I wish the rooster
slept in

Halloween
even the moon vanishes

..

. . .

. . . . . .

into the stepwell

wanting
to bite more than my tongue
Thanksgiving

high school reunion
I watch you dance
to our song

collecting pine cones
the squirrel doesn't understand
why

reminding me
of a distant home
red chinar leaf

in the cracked
porcelain dish
harvest moon

bagpipes blow
in her wake
red leaves fall

bird watching
the neighborhood cat
is quicker

skipping rope
our children
ourselves

rising sun
when old oaks cast
long shadows

blood moon
my ancestors hide
in banyan roots

Sneha Sundaram

empty nest
the leaf blower drowns
our silences

I wish I had laughed more crow's feet

apple picking
the scarecrow's basket
is also full

autumn nights
my imaginary friend
reappears

hunters moon
the ocean swallows
everything

first frost
my garden Buddha
still meditates

WINTER ROSE

filling the gap
between you and I
fresh snow

winter carnival
memories mulled
with wine

bare branches
the water reflects
everything

barbed wire
memories roll in
with the fog

ikebana*
holly berries sparkle
in the snow

* (Japanese) flower arrangement

taking
my secrets with him
melting snowman

Christmas eve
even the birds
fly home

also dissipating
through the fog
bird song

après ski
the beginner tells
the tallest tales

rosebud salve
    some cracks are harder
        to mend

near-sighted
grandpa rues
today's youth

first snow
our footprints disappearing
in the early sun

knit one purl one
some patterns repeat
year after year

thin air
after the big fight
little fights

long before
you walked away
winter moon

through
the deepest fog
light

cold sunshine
I merge into
your shadow

Sneha Sundaram

soaking walnuts
some traditions
I follow

in the middle of the storm snow angels

perigee
I brush the snow
off your lips

first wind in the pines
the table carries the weight
of our resolutions

stolen kisses
the moon trapped
in thin ice

sweater weather
the snowman is also
accumulating snow

you were never
one to shy away
winter rose

fleeting
in baby's little hands
a snowflake

ABOUT THE AUTHOR

Sneha Sundaram is a poet and amateur photographer. Her background is in Engineering (BE, Mumbai University) and Business (MBA, The Pennsylvania State University). Originally from Mumbai, India, she now lives in Jersey City, NJ, USA.

Nature, travel and art inspire her writing.

An accomplished Haiku writer, some of her haiku have been translated to Hindi, German, Italian, Polish, Bulgarian, Croatian and Japanese. Her haiku have also been displayed on the streets of Washington DC as part of the Golden Triangle DC Haiku Contest 2016 and 2017. She won a Sakura award, USA, 2019 in the Vancouver Cherry Blossom Festival. She is also a member of the Haiku Society of America.

Her poems have been published in Asahi Shimbun, Texas Poetry Calendar, Frogpond, Modern Haiku, Noctua Review, Kigo, Whirlwind, JACLR by UC Madrid, Aaduna, Jaggery, Haibun Today, Contemporary Haibun, Sonic Boom, Tinywords, Qu Literary Magazine and several other international publications.

She has won prizes and received commendations in the 20th Kusamakura International Haiku contest, the British Council & Sampad 'Inspired by Museum' poetry contest, Capoliveri International Haiku contest, The 5th Polish International Haiku contest, 2016 Wordweavers Haiku contest, The 2nd International Bulgarian Cherry Blossoms Haiku contest, The Tri Rejeke Croatian International Haiku contest among others.

An exhibition of her Haiku and Photographs, 'A Gingko Walk' will be displayed at the Asian American Resource Center in Austin TX, USA from Jan - Mar 2020.

You can read more about her work at www.snehasundaram.com.

Made in the USA
Lexington, KY
02 November 2019

56323621R00081